RENEWABJ

RENEWABLE ENERGY

The unstoppable power of plants

Edited by Joy Howard

Illustrations: Lizzie Harper

GREY HEN

First published in 2022 by Grey Hen Press
PO Box 269
Kendal
Cumbria
LA9 9FE
www.greyhenpress.com

ISBN   978-1-9196455-1-3

Printed by Flexpress, Birstall, Leicester LE4 3BY

For my sister Francie, with love

Contents

Listen

Waking to silence.
Dark disperses into the held breath
of morning, where the fret of traffic
has slowed into waiting. Walk

into a conspiracy of trees in wind –
the toss of cherry blossom's last
fling, the thrash and snatch of ash, straining
to hear the yew's dark mutterings

woven with the crack of jackdaw, creak
of collared dove, robin's
chinks, wren's pinprick,
muffled scuffle of pigeons. Walk

into a place of soft speech
where a blackbird's cocked head
says listen to the earth....
Now you can hear the unheard –

the shuffle of a slug's slow haul,
fungi's heavy breathing,
leaves letting go, pulled in
by worms' warm words –

you can catch the hidden
gulps and bubbles of heartwood
sucking sap, the gluttonous
green squeak of seedlings. Listen

to the rustle of pages being turned
in the book of this place –
find where you belong, even
just to hold the door open.

Christina Buckton

For Planting

A pebbling
of acorns, beech mast,
bristled sweet chestnuts

sycamore seeds
wide-winged as angels
catch at my hair

there are berries
hawthorn, holly, yew,
the gleam of conkers

the trees
in a stir of wind
toss down their gifts

such possibilities!
I scoop a handful up, hold
a hedgerow, a copse, a wood.

Annette Iles

November Mood Music

The cloudless afternoon starts to fade.
A short pink contrail from over the pole
crawls across the sky to this city or that.
Nothing else moves.

Computer models struggle.
Forecasts are wrong: windless so long
leaves fell straight down, settled
in perfect circles round the trunks.

The magnetic north pole's lurched east.
The planet wobbles closer to drop-off.
I rake up yellow roundels under the hazel,
their fine velvet nap still damp. How to bear

the news? Easier when there were gods
and afterlives. The gold leaves top off the heap
already higher than me: next year's leafmould
for next year's planting – faith of some sort.

Jane Routh

Winter

Winter mists obliterate the skyline.
Stillness in the laden trees.
Ice-fast ground.
Deep quiet of snow.

Bone-cold, the wild rabbit
Crouches between the railway sleepers.
Cat, bewildered, picks his way
Seeking his clump of heather
To relieve himself. Stands listening
Confused by cold.

Not a postcard sky
Grey, brooding,
No longer reflected in the hard pool.
White marks below the ice
Show where the carp died,
Embedded now in the thickening slab.

Winter and despair show the same arrogance,
Claiming the last word.
Where no poems are left
One anachronistic spear of green
Has cheeked its way through the shroud.

Hilary Elfick

Green Shoots

So much of last year's growth now cut back,
and soil, the sustainer, turned over, dug in.
Stirred by cold drenchings, a sudden sun
in a clear sky, beaming hotly down,
tips of green shoots – like blades, packed tightly –
respond to the soil's nutrients,
the changing seasons,
blights, beyond in the larger world.

And as the stem rises, buds of new growth,
still crinkled in a thin papery sheaf,
take on a vibrancy, a particularity of detail,
they organise themselves into a spiral,
ready to grow strongly outwards,
transform, through the flowering seeding cycle.

Sara Boyes

The Yellow Flag Iris

have arrived by the side of our river.
They are pretending
that they've been here forever
which is a lie because I know
they have been blown hither
by a singular light breeze
that knew we were in need
of their staunch, upright stalks,
their hopeful yellow,
their flags unfurling new life.

Diana Hendry

Hum of Bluebells

Half-belled, half-budded, they electrify the wood,
plugged live into sunlight like a million mini-bulbs
coding and glowing in bells of pearled glass.

Each return I'm stunned by the lift and float, the energy
of violet-blue vibrations, radiant from shadow-clearing
blossom that hides winter-mould underfoot.

What force can throw the switch on spring
to power such a surge it makes essential colours hum,
the fragrance of the blue wood zing?

June Hall

Wildflowers on May Day

Glad to be out with a clear sky in spring,
she followed an old lane not much used
and began to search among wild flowers
that leant under hedgerows.
They appeared suddenly on my phone,
image after image, bright, fresh.
The wild into my hands.

She showed me bluebells for constancy
with sorrel for affection, honesty's sincerity,
valerian for strength, snowbell for the blood,
greater stitchwort property of pixies,
fern for humility and some magic too.
Young beech leaves, green for energy flow,
milkmaid for hope in sad times,
red campion to guard against loneliness
and bring in the faeries' blessing.
Found by my daughter, the flowers still shine together.

Rose Cook

Cow Parsley

or Queen Anne's Lace, said my grandmother.
it's a better name: finely matched shapes
of pale filigree held up to let the sun through,
to veil the view behind, but allow light
enough for bluebells and yellow poppies.

Anthriscus sylvestris is its proper name:
a breeze along the verge in June skims
swathes of cream lace as far as you can see,
borders gathered and draped, outspread
to adorn new summer grass; and
disguise barbed wire and discarded cans

Hilary Tattershall

17

Wild Roses

In the Victorian language of flowers
the wild rose signifies pleasure and pain

Carl in the smallholding over the road
lets his hedges tower to the sky.
He has his reasons as the wild roses
and their bees have their seasons. As do I.
The roses take full advantage,
do what they always did in the wildwood
before roads before fields before hedges;
hitch a lift with whatever goes skyward.

I look up where they trail thorny sprays,
pale flowers, frail and fierce like babies.
Seek high, bees. Against the blue of June
with the world awry, why am I, too,
shaken with those white and pink hearts
that scatter and fly with the breeze?

Jo Peters

Field Bindweed
from *The Observer's Book of Wild Flowers*

Stems are numerous, slender and twining

       troublesome

Pink petals   honeyed   scented
entirely unite in a corolla   funnel-shaped
whose folds and lobes indicate
the origin and are

     a favourite

Much frequented by long-tongued insects
night closes its pink cups
as does wet weather
that nectar may not be reduced in quality

      a form of grace

Resisting plucking
the delicately fragrant funnels
entirely united   furl immediately
if touched

     resentful

A creeping rootstock branches   many feet
taking possession of much soil

      perennial

Joy Howard

Rebellion

These dandelions – no show girls
but they know how to pop up
where they're not wanted
go on, do your worst
on tarmac and paving stone
Parliament Square, Waterloo Bridge
padlocked into earth with combination roots
go on, arrest me
not ashamed to flaunt
the green rosette around their petals
rewilding the conurbation
raising the question of offence
with ranks of blue lawnmowers
doing their job, keeping order.

And in the borders, doing what they do
and in orchards and gardens beyond
the healing herbs, berry bushes,
apple and peartrees sending their fruit –
in every open space, every town centre
they're flowering in solidarity
clematis clinging on, geraniums
making a statement, even
under the hedges, a host
of violets quietly clicking send.

Jennie Osborne

Hope

Thistledown be damned.
Nothing is as soft as milkweed, pods
split, redeeming promises of flight.

Skirt-seeds, air-seeds:
a curve of wind confers
upon them its next dance.

Those left behind gathered,
spilt, pressed to wan cheeks:
the hope of a final journey.

Jennifer A McGowan

All Change

Even our small back gardens look confused
seasons no longer make sense to them, roses
in particular find things difficult, decisions
no longer theirs – twig, leaf, bud, bloom, hip –
all come seemingly at random throughout
the year, and not just roses, but spring bulbs
will now rise up and look around in November
shaking their heads as if to ask what the hell
is going on, while my camellias draw lots
as to which of them will open first and
when. But it's also tough for gardeners.
Should we prune, sow, feed, mulch, mow
now or more probably, eight weeks ago?
Simpler to take it easy in shed or sunroom,
merely watching as the weeds take over,
thrive and die – while we tell ourselves
their dead growth provides a perfect habitat
for wildlife. So here we are, promoting
biodiversity by merely doing nothing; it's
a comforting thought and there aren't many.

Angela Kirby

Finale

You millions, I embrace you! This kiss is for the whole world! Schiller

The sea is grey, the air is cold
the yellow sun is missing.

But every day that gorse is gold
the time is right for kissing.

Joy Howard

Ulex (commonly known as gorse, furze, or whin) is noted for being in flower
throughout the year.

23

The Poets

Sara Boyes' poems have appeared in magazines and anthologies since the 80's; she's also published two collections – *Kite and Wild Flowers* from Stride and a pamphlet *Black Flame* from Hearing Eye. For many years she taught creative writing at Birkbeck College. **Christina Buckton** lives near Cambridge. She started writing poetry in her eighties, winning awards at Guernsey, the Candlestick Press, Dempsey and Windle and elsewhere. She has recently published her first collection, *Holding it Together,* with The Lamplight Press. Other poems have appeared in The North, Stand, Orbis and Fenland Journal. **Rose Cook** is a poet based in the South West. She co-founded the popular Devon poetry and performance forum *One Night Stanza*. Her poetry has been published in six collections, her latest book is *Fresh Start: A Shepherd's Calendar (*published by Hen Run, Grey Hen Press 2021). **Hilary Elfick**, broadcaster, is author of twenty two collections of poetry, a musical and a novel. She has performed in cathedrals, theatres, bookshops, galleries, schools and Literary Festivals in many countries including Australasia and Africa. Her books have been featured by postgraduates in London and Bucharest. Her Polynesian interpretation of Shakespeare's *The Tempest* brought considerable interest from the international Shakespeare community. **June Hall** lives in Bath, married to the novelist, Gregory Hall. Her first baby's death and her own diagnosis of Parkinson's in her 40s have contributed to her published collections *The Now of Snow* (2004), *Bowing to Winter* (2010) and *Uncharted* (2016) all with Belgrave Press, and the chapbook *What If?* (Hen Run, Grey Hen Press 2021). **Diana Hendry** has published six collections of poetry, including *The Seed-Box Lantern: New & Selected Poems* (Mariscat). A new collection, *The Guest House,* (Worple Press) is just out. Of her many children's books, *Harvey Angell* won a Whitbread Award and *The Seeing*, was shortlisted for a Costa Book Award. **Joy Howard** loves a reasonably tidy garden is trying hard to allow a bit of the wild to find its place amongst the otherwise tended borders. She particularly enjoys the way her garden plants sneak out into the lane while all kinds of wild plants make the reverse journey. **Annette Iles** is a Midlands-based poet who grew up in rural New Zealand in the 1950s. Her work has appeared in magazines including *Magma, The Cannon's*

Mouth, and *Brittle Star*, as well as a number of anthologies. In 2018 she won the West Midlands *Poetry on Loan* competition. **Angela Kirby** was born (1932) in rural Lancashire, and now lives in London. Her widely published poems have won prizes and commendations in several major competitions, have twice won the BBC Wildlife Poet the Year award, were featured in 'Poetry On the Buses', appeared on TV and Radio 4, and are translated into Romanian. **Jennifer A McGowan**'s sixth collection *How to be a Tarot Card (or a Teenager)* is now out (Arachne Press). In 2020 she won the Prole pamphlet competition with *Still Lives with Apocalypse*, and also won the Scottish mountain writing competition. Not bad for an already-disabled poet, who also in 2020 contracted Covid and has had daily debilitating symptoms of Long Covid ever since. **Jennie Osborne'**s work grapples with the ecological and climate crisis, particularly in her third collection, *Signals From the Other* (Dempsey and Windle 2022). Her two previous collections are from Oversteps Press. She is inspired by performing with musicians and is an organiser of Teignmouth Poetry Festival. **Jo Peters** has been writing poetry for more years than she cares to remember. She has been published in several magazines as well as in many anthologies, and she has had success in a number of competitions. Her pamphlet *Play* and her collection *like yellow like flying* are published by Half Moon Books. **Jane Routh** has published four poetry collections with Smith/Doorstop, and a prose book about the north west environment where she lives. Her work has been shortlisted for a Forward Prize first collection, and received a Poetry Book Society recommendation. **Hilary Tattershall**, born in Wimbledon, has spent most of her life north of the Thames and now lives in Cumbria. On retirement, she started to explore more creative interests, and was fortunate to find Dove Cottage Poets in Grasmere, and Joy Howard (Grey Hen Press) who has included several of Hilary's poems in her anthologies.

Acknowledgements

CHRISTINA BUCKTON 'Listen' *Holding It Together* (The Lamplight Press 2022). ROSE COOK 'Wild Flowers on May Day' published in *Can You Hear the People Sing* (Palewell Press 2020). HILARY ELFICK 'Winter' *The Horse Might Sing* published in *Envoi*. JUNE HALL 'Hum of Bluebells' *Bowing to Winter* (Belgrave Press 2010). JOY HOWARD 'Field Bindweed' *Refurbishment* (Ward Wood Publications 2011), 'Finale' previously published as 'There You Have It' in *Perfect Binding* (Lulu.com 2021). ANGELA KIRBY 'All Change' published online in *Morphrog*. JENNIE OSBORNE 'Rebellion' *Signals From the Other* (Dempsey and Windle 2022). JO PETERS 'Wild Roses' published in *14 magazine*. JANE ROUTH 'November Mood Music' *Listening to the Night* (Smith/Doorstop 2018).

Joy Howard is the founder of Grey Hen Press, which specialises in publishing the work of older women poets. Her poems have featured in many anthologies and journals and can be found online at *poetry p f*. She has edited twenty two previous Grey Hen Press anthologies, and published a collection of her own poems *Exit Moonshine* about her 'coming out' experiences in the 1980s. Her second collection, *Refurbishment*, was published by Ward Wood in 2011 and her third, *Foraging*, by Arachne Press in 2016.

www.greyhenpress.com